BEGINNER'S GUIDE

AQUARIUM SHRIMP

THE HANDBOOK TO BREED, FEED, MAINTAIN AND CARE FOR FRESHWATER SHRIMP IN TANK

AquaHealth

ISBN: 9798873108091
Copyright © by AquaHealth, 2023
All rights reserved

Introduction

Over the years, shrimp have become the favorite invertebrates of aquarists. Their shimmering colors, their peaceful behavior, their relative ease of breeding and their auxiliary quality of "aquarium cleaner" have given shrimps a special place in our aquatic worlds.

Today there are a multitude of species, with very different aspects and needs. As this guide is aimed at beginners, we will focus in this one on the Neocaridina Davidi, the species being by far the most popular and easiest to start with.

We will first see a detailed presentation of this dwarf shrimp, including: its anatomy, its origin, its natural biotope, its way of life, its behavior, its mode of reproduction, etc. All this information will allow us to understand as best as possible the needs of the shrimp, which must be met as much as possible to keep them in optimal health.

We will then see what technical equipment will be required, how to best arrange the aquarium for shrimp, how to introduce them so that they acclimatize perfectly, how to feed them and how to maintain them.

Finally, the last part will offer an overview of the other existing species of shrimp and the requirements and particularities specific to each.

Follow the guide, let's go!

Summary

Neocaridina davidi

Ideal aquarium

Preparation and care

Other species

Neocaridina Davidi

Presentation and origin

Neocaridina Davidi, formerly called *Neocaridina Heteropoda*, like all freshwater shrimps, belongs to the invertebrate family: they lack a spine and have a shell that protects their body. Originating like most shrimp from Asia, it is found over a wide geographical distribution extending from the Korean peninsula to Taiwan, via mainland China and Japan. The first variety selected and also the best known was *Red Cherry*, the original strain of which was developed in Taiwan.

Small but sturdy

The *Neocaridina Davidi* is considered a dwarf shrimp. Its size is on average 2 cm (0,8 inch) and rarely exceeds 3 cm (1,2 inch) for females, larger than males. It has 5 pairs of legs and a segmented shell along its abdomen which ends in a fan-shaped tail, making it a very good swimmer.

However, it is on the ground that it spends most of its time, looking for the slightest food, algae, waste, or micro-organisms to consume. A detritivore, it will thus be almost autonomous in feeding itself, as long as the aquarium contains sufficient natural elements such as plants (in particular aquatic mosses such as Java moss). In addition to its simple diet, *Neocaridina* is very tolerant of water quality levels. It will therefore adapt very well to most running waters.

Shrimp Anatomy

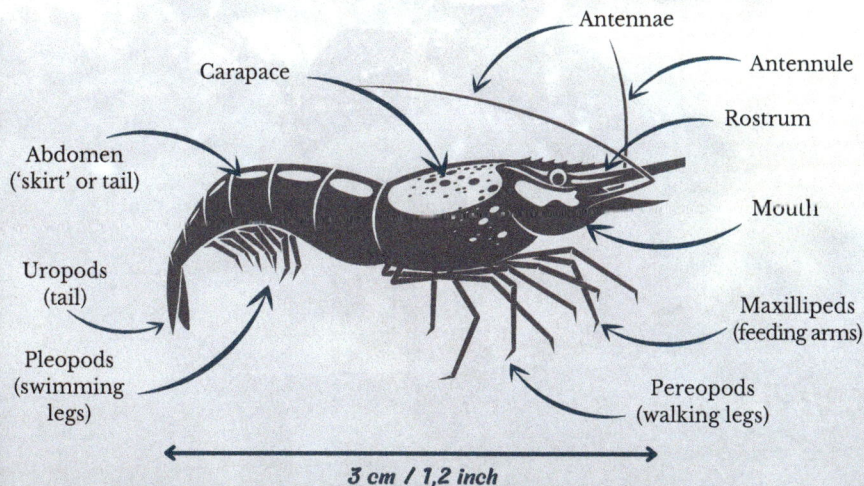

Antennae
Antennule
Carapace
Rostrum
Abdomen ('skirt' or tail)
Mouth
Uropods (tail)
Maxillipeds (feeding arms)
Pleopods (swimming legs)
Pereopods (walking legs)

3 cm / 1,2 inch

Sexual dimorphism

It can be quite difficult for a beginner's eye to discern male and female in shrimp, as the sexual dimorphism is not very pronounced. Only two characteristics differ slightly between individuals of both sexes.

First of all in terms of size : males are generally smaller than females. But the most striking element lies in the shape of the abdomen and the segments constituting it. In the female they extend further, to ensure the protection of the eggs held by the pleopods. Males have a much thinner and slender abdomen.
It is also sometimes possible to observe in females with less opaque colors the ovarian sac (spot shape) located at the top of the carapace, behind the head.

▶ Large plates with wide segments on the abdomen, characteristic of females.

▶ Smaller plates, present in males.

Neocaridina Davidi

Biotope

The Neocaridina, like other species of freshwater aquarium shrimp, originates mainly from Asia. They are found in colonies of several dozen, even hundreds of individuals, at the bottom of rivers and streams that are rather stagnant or not very agitated, in which they remain discreet in order to avoid heavy predation. If the water in these regions has parameters rather neutral, neither too soft nor too hard and neither particularly acidic or basic, it can however undergo significant variations during floods, quickly changing its physico-chemical characteristics. This explains why these shrimp are so tolerant of our aquarium water. In captivity, you will still need to ensure that you have the most stable parameters with as little variation as possible.

In their wild aquatic environment, we find an omnipresent organic mass composed of aquatic plants (especially moss and algae), and a large quantity of dead leaves, roots, and other plant debris. These elements are essential to shrimp since they represent an important part of their diet (especially for juveniles) and allow them to protect themselves from their numerous predators by hiding there.

In its natural state, *Neocaridina Davidi* has a life expectancy of 12 to 18 months. In captivity, it can live up to 18 months, but these durations are largely influenced by the temperature of the water where it lives. The warmer the water, the faster the metabolism will be, therefore the more frequent the molts will be and therefore the more accelerated the aging of the shrimp.

Characteristics of the biotope
The biotope defines all the physical and chemical characteristics of a given environment. For the Neocaridina Davidi biotope :

Low current   Significant vegetation   46 - 75 °F   6 - 8   5 - 15°

Neocaridina Davidi

Varieties and colors

Breeding Neocaridina davidi for over a decade now has resulted in a multitude of patterns and colors. However, all these forms are of the same species and can therefore reproduce with each other. Today there are more than 50 different varieties, making the choice for beginners as complex as understanding this plurality !

To see things more clearly, we will present below the phylogenetic tree of the main colors existing today and perfectly fixed and the procedure to follow if you also wish to recreate or maintain your own strain.

Method : Select and downgrade

If you have already undertaken research on this subject, perhaps you have already come across these two words: selected shrimp and degraded shrimp. To understand the meaning of these terms, we must understand the process leading to a new phenotype (physical appearance) such as a new color, namely: genetic selection. If these terms remind you of a laboratory in which scientists have fun manipulating genes through their microscope to create mutant forms, well... That's not exactly that!

Genetic selection is a methodology carried out directly by the breeder according to his expectations. This is the same method used for absolutely all farmed animal species and for which no direct genetic manipulation takes place. And it's actually very simple.

The breeder will identify in certain individuals of the same species, a notable physical difference, resulting from a natural and random genetic mutation. This may, for example, in the shrimp Neocaridina davidi have a slight red, blue or yellow pigmentation in a normally translucent gray or brown individual.

The first step will therefore consist of selecting these individuals with unique characteristics and then reproducing them among themselves in order to isolate and genetically (but naturally) fix the genes associated with these colored pigments. The reproductions will then be carried out over several generations during which the breeder will systematically make new selections on the new generations, in order to always preserve only those presenting the desired physical characteristics and which will be more and more pronounced. The individuals excluded from the selection will be the "downgraded" individuals.

Strains and selections

All current colors are not obtained according to the same artificial selections. Below, four diagrams representing the selections, also called "grades", allowing the current main colors to be obtained. Associated names are unofficial terms, but often used in commerce. They can therefore vary depending on the interlocutors. To better understand them, some explanations of the names used :

Sakura : Opaque color
Fire : Intense color
Rili : Two-tone body with generally translucent abdomen
Neon : Line across the entire back ranging from yellow to brown

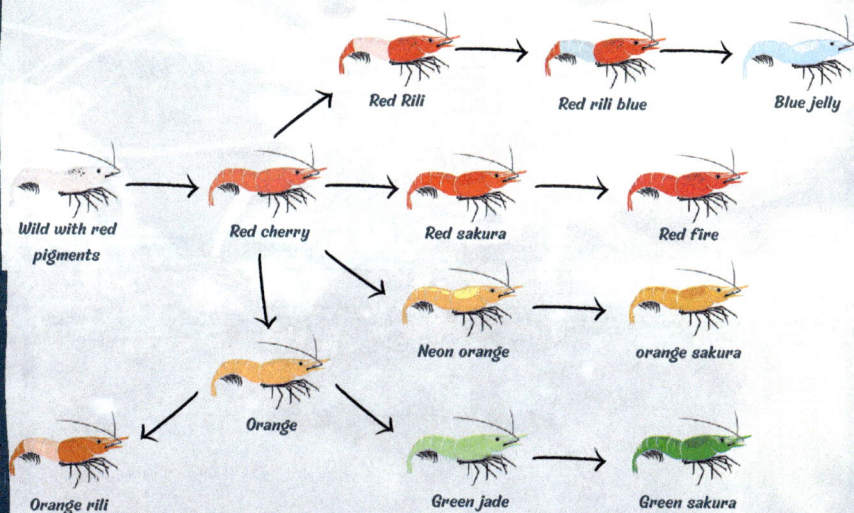

"Red strain"

Red Rili → Red rili blue → Blue jelly

Wild with red pigments → Red cherry → Red sakura → Red fire

Neon orange → orange sakura

Orange

Orange rili

Green jade → Green sakura

"Yellow strain"

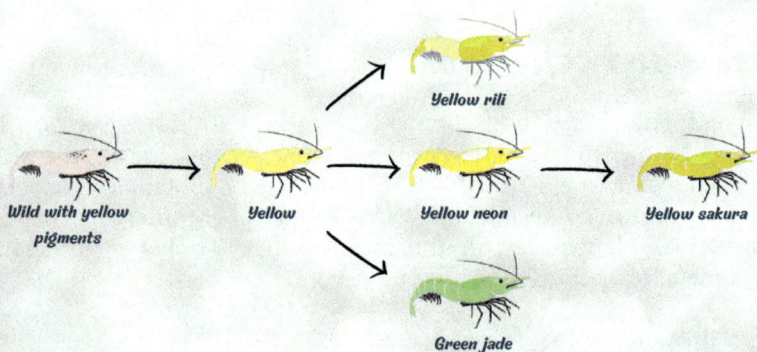

Wild with yellow pigments → Yellow → Yellow rili

Yellow → Yellow neon → Yellow sakura

Yellow → Green jade

"Blue strain"

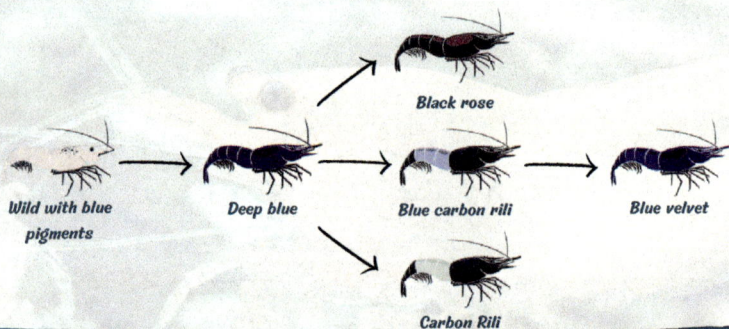

Wild with blue pigments → Deep blue → Black rose

Deep blue → Blue carbon rili → Blue velvet

Deep blue → Carbon Rili

"Brown strain"

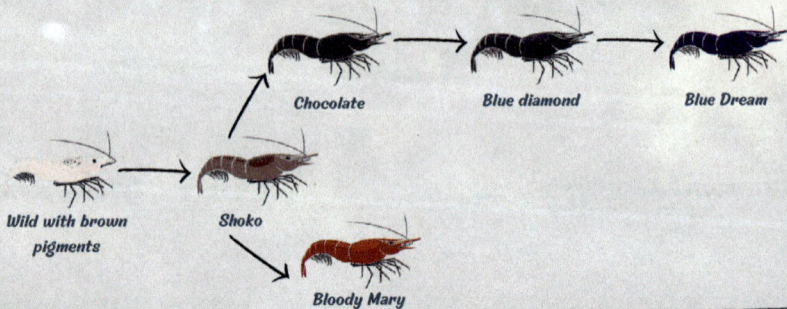

Wild with brown pigments → Shoko → Chocolate → Blue diamond → Blue Dream

Shoko → Bloody Mary

Neocaridina Davidi

Molting and reproduction

Like any invertebrate, shrimp need to molt throughout their life, depending on their growth. This phenomenon allows them in particular to replace their shell when it becomes too small for their body. In order to facilitate this process, it will be necessary to ensure that the Neocaridinas are provided with a correctly balanced diet and sufficiently carbonated water (KH > 3) to build their new shell.

Reproduction is closely linked to the moulting period. Indeed, the end of the moult in the female marks the moment when she is fertilizable. At this moment, the males present will move in all directions (we say they "dance") until they briefly land on the turned over female shrimp to fertilize the eggs. The act is very fast and lasts only a few seconds. Once fertilized, the ovarian sac descends from the back to the underside of the abdomen. We then speak of a grained female. The eggs (around forty at each laying) will thus be preserved and ventilated by the female thanks to her pleopods throughout their incubation period, of approximately 3 to 4 weeks. They will give birth to perfectly formed and autonomous little transparent ones called juveniles (and not zoeas!). They will move and feed in the same way as adult shrimp. In the absence of predators in the aquarium, they will reach adulthood without problem.

A complete and varied diet (see part - Food - page 38), healthy water with suitable parameters (see part - Water - page 22) and a high temperature of 72 to 75°F, will be all elements which will encourage shrimp to reproduction.

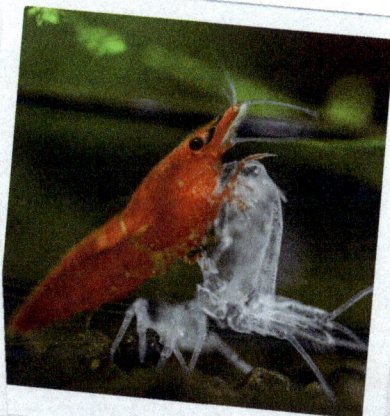

▲ A grained female on the left and one in full molt on the right !

Neocaridina Davidi

Cohabitation

Shrimp are not solitary animals. They are gregarious animals that need to live in small colonies made up of at least ten individuals. It will therefore always be necessary to keep them in groups.

Inter-species cohabitation

There is no form of competition, territoriality or predation in Neocaridina and freshwater shrimp species in general. We can thus mix males, females and juveniles without any problem without worrying about cohabitation between them. However, you should avoid mixing the different colors if you want to preserve your strains. In fact, the different variants will hybridize, eventually producing individuals with wild gray/brown colors.

Cohabitation with other species

Shrimp are totally peaceful animals and rather fearful, rightly so! Invertebrates are the natural prey of a number of other species, including most fish. It is possible to achieve long-term cohabitation with certain fish (such as Corydoras, small Tetra, Danio, Ancistrus or Otocinclus) if the volume of the aquarium is suitable.

For the rest, this remains possible but we must expect systematic predation of juveniles (therefore limited reproduction) and less flourishing shrimp, becoming very discreet and difficult to observe.

▶ Shrimp and their behavior are only perfectly observable in specific tanks !

Ideal aquarium

Before even thinking about buying shrimp, you need to think about and prepare the aquarium that will accommodate them. This point is the most important because it is the one which will define the quality and lifespan of your future arrivals. We will see that shrimp are very undemanding in terms of habitat. However, certain criteria must be respected to ensure their well-being.

The first question to ask yourself is whether you want to keep our shrimp alone, in a specific tank or in a community tank with other species of invertebrates and/or fish. Please note that the specific tank will be better suited if you want to carefully observe your shrimp and optimize reproduction. In a community tank reproduction will be more complicated because of the predation exerted by most fish on juvenile shrimp (but not impossible). The other advantage is that the specific tank can be of a more modest size (nanoaquarium style) while a community tank must be much larger (at least 20 gal) to ensure sufficient space for each individual.

In this part we will deal with shrimp maintenance in specific tanks only. The advice provided, however, remains generally valid for community maintenance.

Examples of nanoaquariums suitable for shrimp alone

Ideal aquarium

The tank

The choice of tank is not of capital importance as shrimp are small crustaceans which spend the majority of their time finding food on the ground or on the decor. They therefore do not need a great swimming length, which is normally allowed thanks to the rectangular shape of the aquarium. We can therefore turn either to this shape of tank, having a larger floor area and a lower height (to be preferred in most cases) or a square shape with a smaller surface area, but whose height will be more important. In this second option, it will be necessary to create a decoration on several levels (using decorative elements or plants) in order to increase the exploration surface. We will see the types of developments that can be made in the section - Development - page 32.

Although shrimp do not need much space, you will still need to provide them with a tank with a minimum volume of 20 liters net for a group of around ten individuals. This may seem like a lot for such a small number, but such a volume makes it possible to anticipate a little better future reproductions which are very prolific and which will increase the population of the tank very quickly in the case of optimal maintenance.

Also note that the smaller the volume of the tank, the more difficult the parameters (especially the temperature in summer !) will be to stabilize.

Possible types of tanks

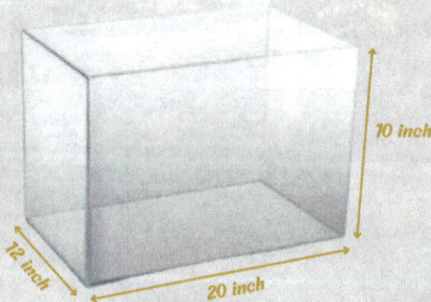

10 inch

12 inch

20 inch

Rectangle

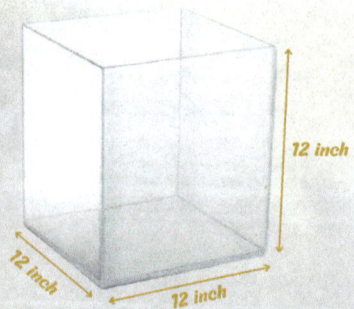

12 inch

12 inch

12 inch

Cubic

Ideal aquarium

Technical equipment

In the case of a specific shrimp aquarium, the technical equipment may be more or less minimalist. We will see that several configurations are possible depending on your expectations and your budget.

Standard equipment

Heating to ensure a certain temperature.

Lighting to simulate day/night diurnal cycles, important for the behavior of animals and especially for the good growth of plants.

A pump equipped with filter masses to avoid stagnation and pollution of water.

These elements are generally essential for a classic aquarium, containing more or less complex species of fish in terms of maintenance, but not for shrimp. In their absence, we speak of a "low-tech" baccalaureate.

For example, we can refrain from using a heater if the aquarium is in a sufficiently warm room (above 70°F). Shrimp tolerate a relatively wide temperature range, ranging from 42°F to 82°F. The optimal temperature, however, is around 70/72°F. A water temperature of 73/75°F boosts reproduction, but in return reduces the lifespan of the shrimp.

The classic filter can also be substituted in certain cases, due to the low pollution produced by shrimp. However, its absence is not recommended if you are starting out.

Finally, even if artificial lighting is also in no way vital for shrimps which would be satisfied with natural lighting, it is necessary for living plants and their growth.

Now let's see all this in detail.

Filtration

Filtration is not vital for shrimp but it contributes to the biological balance of the aquarium. In other words, it helps maintain a healthy and viable environment for your invertebrates by relieving you of certain maintenance tasks (less regular water changes). It is therefore rather recommended when you are starting out to avoid any risk, even if it is entirely possible to do without it.

Filtration mainly allows water to be purified and purified of its waste in different ways.
Firstly, mechanically, by sucking up and trapping the detritus and particles present in suspension in the aquarium. Also in a biological way, by allowing the degradation of all toxic chemical compounds (from organic waste) into other compounds less dangerous for aquatic life (what is called the nitrogen cycle, see part - Water - page 22). A third filtration, called chemical, can be used but for specific needs only (such as to eliminate drug residues after treatment or to intervene on certain chemical parameters of the water for example).
It also oxygenates the water by creating slight swirls on the surface of the water, promoting gas exchange.

In any aquarium, filtration will have these same very important functions for the good health of the tank and its inhabitants.
For this, however, it must have certain characteristics:

Suitable filter materials : you may have already noticed that filters are often made up of "foam" and filter materials of different appearances and colors. This does not meet an aesthetic criterion but a technical one. Certain foams are thus intended for mechanical filtration (white wadding or blocks of large mesh foam, generally blue), others intended for biological filtration (often solid and porous material in the form of small gravel, balls or noodles such as pozzolan, ceramic, clay, etc.) Finally, those allowing chemical purification are often black foam blocks of activated carbon.

Your filter must be composed of elements allowing mechanical filtration on the one hand and elements allowing biological filtration on the other hand.

➡ **A suitable flow rate** : Shrimp are not big polluters like fish. It is therefore not necessary to use a pump with very high flow rates in the case of a specific shrimp aquarium. 1 to 2 times the volume of the aquarium per hour will be more than sufficient. For a 8 gal aquarium, a filter set at a minimum to obtain a flow rate of 16 gal / h will be suitable.

➡ **A secure filter intake** : The strainer is the part of the pump where the water is sucked. Depending on the type of pump used, some modifications may be necessary. In fact, traditional pumps generally do not pose a problem for adult shrimp which are large enough not to be sucked through the openings of the strainers. However, juveniles are much more at risk.

There are strainer with much finer mesh, which can be purchased commercially and which can be mounted directly on the pump. You can also make your own system using women's stockings or perlon-type filtration foam to place on the intake (see following example).

It is strongly recommended to secure the suction of your pumps if you want to see the juveniles of your reproductions grow !

Types of filter that can be used :

Internal filter	Waterfall filter	Enhancer filter
➕ Silent Filtration volume Discreet ➖ Clutter a "useful" volume in tank Maintenance	➕ Does not clutter the volume Maintenance ➖ Noisy (it is aptly named Cascade) Not discreet	➕ Low current Suitable for small volumes Price ➖ Slightly noisy Unsightly Provide for the purchase of an air pump (rarely supplied)

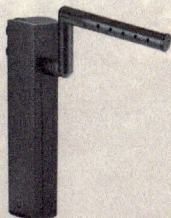

Note : once in place in the aquarium, the filter must rotate continuously without being disconnected. It will be only during the maintenance of the aquarium.

Example of securing the suction of an internal filter

Bare intake

Suction blocked thanks to the perlon

The use of perlon (filtering wadding) makes it possible to seal the gaps and the suction strainer, in order to block access to the juveniles. This example is effective but requires a regular change (once a week) to avoid an excessive reduction in flow rate due to the accumulation of waste at this level.

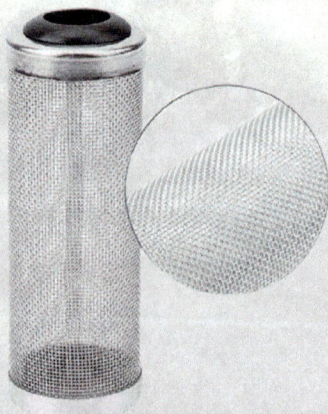

▲ Example of strainer protection

Lighting

Lighting provides two major functions. It first makes it possible to artificially recreate a diurnal cycle, day/night. Many biochemical and metabolic processes depend on these cycles and regulate the behavior of shrimp. If the cycles are disrupted or irregular, this can disturb the animals and gradually create latent stress affecting their good health. Natural plants also have specific light requirements that are more or less demanding depending on their type. It will then be necessary to turn to an artificial lighting system for them.

To be suitable, lighting must meet certain criteria :

➡ **Type** : Neon lights, low consumption bulbs or LEDs. All three can be used but today we mainly find LED ramps on the market. The latter have the advantage of consuming less electricity, having a longer lifespan and heating less for an equivalent light output.

➡ **The power (in W) or the quantity of light (in Lumen) for Leds** : it depends solely on the level of vegetation desired in your aquarium. 0,5W or 25 Lumens per liter of water is a good average. For a very planted tank it will take more with ~ 1W or 40 Lumens / liter.

Regardless of the lighting system, it will be connected to a timer which will automate the switching on and off of the light at a fixed time. The cycles must be continuous.

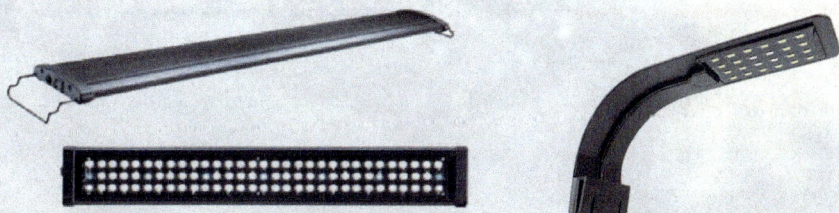

We can use lighting in the form of a ramp with LEDs (left) for aquariums with a significant length or LEDs on a pole (right) for nano-aquariums.

Ideal aquarium

The water

Water is the most important element in the shrimp aquarium, even before the volume or layout of the aquarium (without meaning that these other two points should be neglected!).
It is the one that will alone define the comfort and lifespan of your animals. For this, the chemical composition and quality of the water must be perfect. And these require compliance with the various parameters presented below.

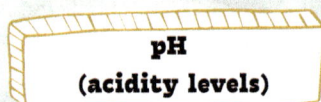

pH
(acidity levels)

pH measures the acidity level of a liquid. It ranges from 0 to 14 and the more its value tends towards 0, the more we will speak of an acidic environment. For example, sodas have a pH around 3. On the contrary, the more the pH value tends towards 14, the more we will speak of an alkaline (or basic) environment. Between these two extreme values, that is to say around ~7, the pH will be described as neutral.
Shrimp such as Neocaridina davidi must be kept in water with a pH between 6.5 and 7.5.
Beyond the value (as long as it is within this reasonable range) it is the sudden variations which will be the most dangerous for the animals (valid for ph but also for any other parameter such as temperature). When traveling to different waters, acclimatization must not be neglected (see section - Acclimatization - page 37)

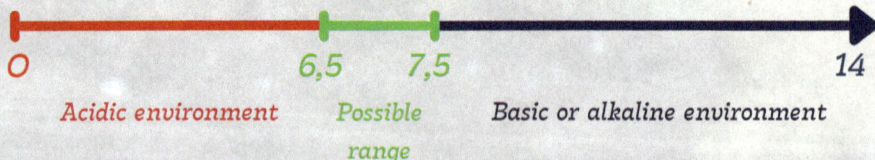

0	6,5	7,5	14
Acidic environment	*Possible range*	*Basic or alkaline environment*	

The tests
You can test your water yourself by purchasing your own kits, but these are often expensive. The other solution may be to take a sample of your aquarium water to a pet store to have them perform the test for you. Most agree to do it for free. Unfortunately, they are often carried out using strips, containing reagents and on which a drop of water from the aquarium is placed. The disadvantage of this type of test is that they are imprecise or even completely wrong. Instead, you should ask for tests in the form of drops to be poured into a precise quantity of aquarium water and whose color change will provide precisely the desired value.

CO2, KH and pH

These three parameters are directly linked to each other. This can be observed in particular in the case of heavily planted aquariums, without CO2 input. In the event of insufficient CO2 in the water, plants draw their necessary carbon from hydrogen carbonate ions, which mechanically lowers the KH value. This phenomenon is called biogenic decalcification. It is recognized in particular by the presence of white spots on the plastics of the filter or the suction cups then on the leaves of the plants when the condition becomes critical. What follows is a sudden increase in pH which can be fatal to the aquarium and its inhabitants.

Biogenic decalcification highlights the existing interaction between CO2, KH and pH. We observe in fact that when the CO2 content varies (here decrease linked to absorption by plants) we also directly vary the KH (downwards) and the PH (upwards). This is because pH mainly results from the combination between KH and CO2. When there is not enough carbon provided by CO2 for plants, they use a secondary source : hydrogen carbonate ions. By being absorbed, these decrease (the KH) and therefore naturally lower the buffering power of the water which in turn allows significant variations in pH.

There are thus optimal values between pH and KH to respect for a perfect balance. For example, having a pH of 6.3 with a KH of 4 would not be suitable in most cases, because the concentration of CO2 present would be too high for fish life.
The value of KH must always be interpreted according to that of pH.

The optimal pH parameters that can be obtained depending on the KH :

KH	pH
1	[6.1 and 6.6]
2	[6.3 and 6.7]
3	[6.5 and 6.9]
4	[6.6 and 7.1]
5	[6.7 and 7.2]
6	[6.8 and 7.3]
7	[6.9 and 7.3]

If with your KH you have pH values lower than those given in the previous table, this means that there is too much CO_2 in the water.

On the contrary, if you have pH values higher than those given above, it means that there is too much O_2 and not enough CO_2. Once this correlation is understood, you can easily vary your pH by first adjusting your KH (by cutting your water with water with a lower KH) then by regulating the CO_2 intake.

Oxygen (O2) and CO2

In a simpler way to understand, the amounts of oxygen and carbon dioxide are also directly related to each other : the greater one, the less the other. We must therefore ensure that we maintain a certain balance between the two with enough CO_2 for the plant part of the tank and enough O_2 for the animals (here our shrimp).

If the container contains significant vegetation, a CO_2 injection system may prove useful to ensure optimal plant growth (as well as if you wish to plant plants with more demanding needs such as red plants, only possible with powerful lighting and a high level of CO_2).

There are many possibilities for implementing such a system, which can be purchased directly from stores or can even be manufactured by oneself (tutorial available on the internet by searching for "artisanal CO_2").

However, before embarking on this project, you must ensure that you have understood the different chemical interactions taking place in the water and correctly size the system (good number of bubbles / minute) in order to have the appropriate quantity of CO_2. for the aquarium without detrimentally adjusting the other parameters.

Water problem

When faced with a major water problem, the first reflex to adopt is to react quickly by replacing a significant quantity of aquarium water with new, healthy water. The second step is to determine that it may be the cause of the problem in order to avoid a recurrence (population level adapted to the size of the tank, cycling of the aquarium, regular maintenance, etc.) A cause often neglected and However, it is common to analyze new water used for water changes. If this is running tap water, your parameter problems may come from there !

Ammonia (NH3), Nitrite (NO2) and Nitrate (NO3)

This trio of molecules composed of nitrogen (N) forms the nitrogen cycle. This phenomenon is one of the most important to know and respect in aquariums. If you have studied a little chemistry in your life, you must have probably already heard the famous quote from Lavoisier :

"Nothing is lost, nothing is created, everything is transformed".

The nitrogen cycle is a principle in aquarium keeping that is based verbatim on this quote. It represents the process of degradation of different organic waste (fish excrement, food remains, plant residues, etc.) which are successively transformed into various chemical substances under the action of bacteria. First in ammonium, then in nitrites and finally in nitrates which will in turn be partly absorbed by the vegetation. If the first two molecules are very toxic for fish, they are a little less so for crustaceans such as shrimp. Conversely, you will need to be more vigilant with nitrates, to which shrimp are much more sensitive than fish.

This cycle represents the biological filtration of the aquarium and requires the presence of good bacteria. However, these bacteria need a certain time and suitable supports to develop. Hence the presence of the filter masses mentioned in the filtration section such as pozzolan, ceramic noodles or any type of porous material favoring the fixation and colonization of bacteria.

You must wait at least 3 to 4 weeks after putting a new tank in water to add living beings, so that the bacteria can set up this cycle !

Optimal values and tolerable maximums for each substance :

Ammonia (NH3) : 0 ppm and 0.1 ppm, if ammonia is present in your tank this means that it has either not been cycled correctly or that a profound imbalance has occurred killing good bacteria.

-> You must start the cycling process again by moving the animals or changing 50% of the water every 2 days (leaving the filtration running).

Nitrites (NO2) : 0 ppm and 0.2 ppm, if the nitrite level exceeds 0.2 ppm they can become fatal for shrimp. A water change of at least 30% every 2 days is recommended until it drops to 0.2 ppm.

Nitrates (NO3) : Up to 10 ppm and 30 ppm. Nitrates are necessary for plants that feed on them. However, beyond a certain level, they become very toxic to shrimp and promote the proliferation of algae. From 30 ppm, a water change of at least 30% must be carried out (check that the replacement water contains little nitrates).

Ideal aquarium

The decoration

The decoration of your bin depends only on you and your tastes. It will still be important for the shrimp to provide them with a safe environment during molts thanks to the hiding places and to allow the development of microfauna on which they can feed. But also important for the benefits it can bring to the ecosystem of your tank. Let's take a look at the different possible elements.

Plants

Focus on natural plants as much as possible! I hate (and I weigh my words carefully) artificial plants, made of fabric or plastic. They only have defects and have nothing to do in an aquarium supposed to recreate a piece of nature.

Of course, natural plants are more demanding and require (a little) more effort in terms of maintenance, but that is nothing compared to the benefits they provide :

- biologically balance the water (consume nitrates, CO2 and oxygenate the water)
- slow down the development of algae by competing with them (both consume the same nutrients)
- offer a source of food thanks to the microfauna that develops there
- are much more aesthetic (this point is purely subjective and only affects individual tastes, but all the same...)

Need for plants

Good light of sufficient quality and quantity is essential (see section - Lighting - page 21). It will be necessary to light little for the first weeks (~7 hours per day) to gradually reach 10/12 hours of lighting per day (30 minutes to 1 hour of additional lighting per week from the second week is a good compromise in my experience) .

Provide all the necessary nutrients (iron, copper, potassium, calcium, etc.) thanks to a nutrient substrate placed under neutral soil, technical soil or via the addition of regular fertilizers (in the form of balls or liquid).

Choice of plants

Next comes the choice of plants. To make the container harmonious, you need to diversify the plants between large plants in the background, moderately sized plants for the middle and small plants for the foreground. Their choice must also be made according to the characteristics of your aquarium: its size obviously but especially the lighting. If you do not have a very high light intensity, you will then have to turn to relatively undemanding plants. Finally, among these, it will also be necessary to make a mix between fast-growing plants (to limit the parallel development of algae) and slow-growing plants (so as not to exhaust nutrients such as CO_2 too quickly).

Below is a small list of plants suitable for getting started :

Slow growing plants

- Cryptocorynes (e.g. *wendtii*, *parva* or *affinis*)

- Java fern (*microsorum pteropus*)

- Anubias

- Bucephalandras

Fast growing plants

- Echinodorus (*Bleher*)

- Hygrophilas (*polysperma*, *corymbosa*, *difformis*)

- African water fern (*bolbitis heudelotii*)

- Elodea (*Egeria densa*)

- *Ceratophyllum demersum*

Finally, an essential plant for shrimp : aquatic mosses like java moss (taxiphyllum barbieri). Shrimp love these moss which they use to feed and hide (especially juveniles).

> **Rhizome plants**
> Some plants have rhizomes, this is particularly the case with anubias and the java fern. For this type of epiphytic plants, you should not bury the rhizome (the root) in the substrate but hang it (using nylon thread, fishing line, sewing or glue) to a root or a stone .

Plant care

To live and have normal growth, plants have specific needs: an adequate temperature, sufficient light supply, water with appropriate parameters (PH, KH, GH, CO2) and nutrients in the right quantity, neither too much nor not enough (Nitrate, Phosphate, Potassium, Iron, Copper, etc.)

There are two types of deficiency in particular, which can explain the delay in growth or death of a plant :

- Deficiency due to the absence of a necessary nutrient, which is the easiest to remedy with appropriate fertilization.
- Induced deficiency, due to impossible assimilation of a type of nutrient by the plant.

This happens in the case of an unbalanced pH (outside the range 6 - 8) or an imbalance linked to the quantity of elements present (example : too many nitrates, too much light, not enough iron, potassium, etc.).

Nutrients are mainly provided by water. But a supplement by the use of a technical soil or the addition of a nutrient soil under a neutral soil (see section - The substrate - page 30) or by adding liquid fertilizer directly to the water, can be beneficial or even essential to certain demanding plants!

Beyond these elements, maintenance will boil down to pruning the plants when the need arises: cutting damaged leaves, covered with algae or that have become too invasive. In these tasks, shrimp prove to be very good allies by taking care of some of the waste!

▶ Red fire removing algae from a leaf.

The substrate

Substrate is the material that is placed at the bottom to make up the floor of the aquarium. It will provide shrimp with an area to explore for food and allow plants to take root. It also represents an important support in the biological balance of the tank since it will house a whole colony of bacteria that purify the water.

Although there is no particular need to be careful about the different substrates that can be used, you still need to know the characteristics of each existing one, in order to choose the one/those that are best suited to your shrimp:

➜ **Porous substrates** : Generally crushed volcanic rock or clay pebbles. This type of substrate is very interesting to use as a first layer of soil. It makes it easy to add volume and drain the soil and thanks to its porosity it allows good rooting of plants and an important bacteriological refuge for the biological purification of water. A generous layer can / should be used.

➜ **Neutral substrates** : This soil can be of different types (Loire sand, quartz, basalt, etc.) and is qualified as neutral because of its particularity in not modifying anything in the tank (nor modifying the water parameters , nor nutrients for plants). Its interest is purely aesthetic, in particular via the different color intensities available (ranging from very light white to very dark black). Best used with nutrient soil underneath to provide nutrients to plants

➜ **Aqua soil** : This is terracotta reconstituted in the form of pellets and containing numerous nutrients for plants. It is called sometime "technical" because when it is used with reverse osmosis water, it interacts directly with the pH by making the water slightly acidic combined with a very low hardness. These modifications are necessary for certain shrimp species (see section - Other species - page 44) but not very much for the Neocaridinas which need a sufficiently high KH.

▲ The different types of substrate with from left to right : crushed lava rock, sand and aquasoil.

Stones, roots and other decorative elements

The main purpose of these elements is to make your bin aesthetic. They can occasionally serve as hiding places, especially during moulting periods, but the shrimp remain rarely hidden in a specific tank. The choice of decorations depends only on your tastes but to avoid certain setbacks, you will have to take some precautions.

➡ **Roots** can be purchased or collected from the wild. In both cases (but particularly the second) you will need to make sure not to introduce harmful elements (fungi, bacteria, parasites, etc.) into your tank, which could accompany the roots. Staying in boiling water for one to two hours will eliminate any potential risk. In addition, this operation will fill the roots with water in order to make them sink more easily (if this is not enough, weight them with a stone for example, until they no longer float) and evacuate a good part of the tannins responsible for the amber coloring of the water. Note that it is normal to observe the development of white mold on them during the first weeks. They will be eaten quickly by the shrimp.

➡ **Stones**, like roots, can be bought or collected. However, for these you will need to find out about their type (limestone to avoid, granite, slate, schist, volcanic, etc.). The stones that you collect yourself must be rubbed, scraped and ideally boiled to remove them. potential unwanted guests.

➡ **The other elements** can be diverse and varied. Natural is best, like coconut halves providing good hiding places. Ceramic tubes are also available on the market, which are very popular with invertebrates. You can also add dry plants such as dry tree leaves (commercially available catappa, oak, birch, etc.) or alder fruits. All these elements add a natural aspect of the most beautiful effect to the tank and contribute to biological balance.

▲ Natural elements with in order : catappa leaf, oak leaf, alder fruit

Ideal aquarium

The layout

Setting up a shrimp aquarium is not very complex, it only needs to follow a few instructions. As we have seen, shrimp swim little. It is then necessary to maximize flat surfaces (on the ground or above ground) to allow their pedestrian movements. It is also necessary to provide enough hiding places to reassure shrimp with rather fearful behavior. It is then necessary to organize all the elements constituting the aquarium in order to meet these needs.

Floor space

First rule when arranging your tank: preserve a good part of the bare ground from all decorations. A third of the total free surface area is a good ratio and this space placed at the front will also make it easy to observe your shrimp. They must be able to walk and search the ground without hindrance. You can still place leaves or dried fruits there (see previous page) which will provide an even more enriching exploration area for the shrimp (they can use them to hide or feed).

▲ Clear ground space, circled in red.

Setting up hiding places

You must then create the hiding places using the elements constituting the decor (stones and roots which constitute what we call the "hardscape" as well as the plants). These hiding places must provide shady places, reassuring for the shrimp. There are no specific rules to follow, you just need to ensure that everything is stable so as not to present a risk of landslides.

▲ Hiding places created by stacking rocks, plants (java fern in the background on the right, anubia nana and cryptocoryne in front of the left) and a root.

Optimize volume

One thing that is regularly neglected is the possibility of optimizing the volume of its tank thanks to the layout, in order to exploit it to the maximum (especially for the small volumes of nanocubes). Stemmed plants with large leaves (such as some presented in the section - Plants - page 27) are the simplest way to achieve this. The shrimp will walk around on these. It is also possible to increase the exploration surfaces thanks to the decorative elements, provided that the appropriate shapes are selected. The roots are therefore better suited to this function as can be seen in the photo below.

The shape and arrangement of the root in the aquarium above makes it possible to add almost 50% additional surface area. This is possible thanks to the three root support points, occupying very little floor space and thus forming a clear "ground floor" and an additional "floor". The shaded part under the root also allows the technical equipment (filter) to be subtly hidden while leaving a free surface for the shrimp.

This arrangement obviously represents an example of what it is possible to do by combining aesthetics (even if this point is purely subjective and specific to each person) and adapting it for the maintenance of shrimp.

It is up to you and your imagination to opt for a different and equally effective arrangement of the bin !

Ideal aquarium

Set up

Below is a table summarizing the equipment to be provided depending on the size of your tank :

Dimensions (inch)	Volume	Tank weight	Lighting	Heating (if necessary)	Filtered	Substrat	Total weight
10 x 12 x 12	6 gal	3 kg	10 W or 500 Lumens	25 W	12 g / hour	6 kg	28 kg
12 x 12 x 13	8 gal	5 kg	15 W or 750 Lumens	50 W	16 g / hour	9 kg	39 kg
20 x 10 x 12	10 us gal	6 kg	20 W or 1000 Lumens	50 W	20 g / hour	12 kg	52 kg

A completely filled aquarium weighs a certain amount, even in the case of a nano aquarium. Make sure you place it on a piece of furniture that can support it, perfectly straight and in a suitable location so that you don't have to move it later.
Likewise, always place a flexible element between the aquarium and the support (carpet style, yoga mat or expanded polystyrene at least 2cm thick) which will absorb the irregularities of the support and prevent the aquarium from breaking under its own weight. Plastic supports to be placed under the four corners of the aquarium are also possible.

An ideal location is in any room of the house except the kitchen and the bathroom (vapours, fumes from grease and cosmetic products are harmful to aquatic life).
You should also avoid placing the aquarium in direct contact with the sun's rays, which could encourage the proliferation of green algae and cause the temperature to rise dangerously in summer.

Cycle start

Here is your tank set up and all your equipment is working correctly. It is now necessary to start the nitrogen cycle (see part - water - page 22) before any introduction of shrimp.

In reality, the cycle starts by itself as soon as the tank is filled with water, with the first waste produced by the plants. But to further initiate this first step, which consists of developing the first bacteria transforming ammonia into nitrites, you can add a slight pinch of food to the water.
A technique consisting of artificially seeding the aquarium is also possible. It consists of introducing these famous bacteria already developed into the aquarium by two different methods:

You can either recover part of the filter masses from a healthy tank already cycled and put them in your own filtration. In this way, bacteria from the other aquarium will colonize your tank more quickly.
You can also buy vials of ready-to-use bacteria directly from the store. Personally, I am not a fan of this method, as it offers no guarantee on the quality and effectiveness of the bacteria that will be introduced.

These two methods theoretically speed up the cycle for the most impatient, but it is also possible (and recommended) to let nature take its course and wait three to four weeks while the bacteria naturally colonize the aquarium. Regardless of the method chosen, one step will remain essential: regularly check the parameters of your water and particularly the level of nitrites and nitrates. These are the values that will give the green light for the introduction of your shrimp, when they have reached a higher level to finally approach 0 mg/l.

Waste (food, droppings, ...)

NH4 AMMONIUM

NO2 NITRITE

NO3 NITRATE

Nitrogen cycle in the aquarium : under the effect of various bacteria, the waste is transformed into NH4, the NH4 is degraded into NO2 then the NO2 into NO3. NO3 is then consumed by plants (and algae).

Preparation

Acclimatization

Once you have purchased your shrimp, try not to delay bringing them home in order to limit the stress caused (in case you buy them in a pet store). Note that juveniles generally tolerate transport better than adults.

Upon arrival, the first thing you should definitely not do is transfer your shrimp directly with the water from the bag into your aquarium. Not knowing the quality of the water your shrimp comes from, it is safer to throw it away to avoid risking any future contamination of your tank.
Likewise, the parameters and temperature of the two waters are undoubtedly very different, it will be necessary to proceed with slow and progressive acclimatization to avoid any shock. Concerning shrimp, you should favor the "drip by drop" method explained below:

➡ Open the transport bag using a pair of scissors if necessary, and pour the contents (water + shrimp) into a sufficiently large container. This can be a salad bowl or a plastic bucket. Just make sure it is clean and has never contained any chemicals or household products. A volume of 2/3 liters will be necessary.

➡ Then place the container containing the shrimps near the future aquarium, but slightly lower than it (on a chair for example). You will then need to use a hose (silicone air hose type, supplied with the air pumps if you have one or purchased separately at a pet store) with a length of at least 1 to 2 meters. It will be necessary to equip one of the ends of the latter with either a small plastic tap (also supplied with the air pumps or purchased separately) or to tie a knot in the pipe itself in order to reduce the flow. You will need to adjust the tap or tighten the knot more or less to obtain approximately 2 drops/second. We will then place this end in the container containing the shrimp and the other in the aquarium by sucking, to transfer the water by siphoning.

➡ You will then need to fill the shrimp container until the initial volume of water has tripled. This indication is approximate and it is not necessary to precisely measure the quantity of water poured which may be more or less significant. Once enough water has been poured from the aquarium into the container, you can add the shrimp to the aquarium. A fine mesh landing net will allow you to catch the shrimp without hurting them and release them into the tank.

Care and maintenance

Food

Shrimp are omnivores, mainly alguivores and detritivores. They feed on any organic "waste" (plants, dead fish or other shrimp) but also on algae and different microorganisms present in an aquarium. However, their diet will need to be supplemented with other foods.

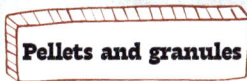

Pellets and granules

This is the most common type of food. Dry food, such as pellets or pellets, should be used as a staple food for shrimp.

There are a multitude of products available on the market, of more or less equivalent quality. You

▲ Example of shrimp pellets

can turn to pellets specifically intended for shrimp, but also those intended for other invertebrates (crayfish, crabs, etc.) or even use pellets for tropical fish. "Lollies" (lollipops in English) which are sticks covered with different dried foods, are a very fashionable treat because they are very popular with shrimp, which can be given to them occasionally (once a week maximum).

Concerning distribution, a few granules 3/4 times a week are generally sufficient. You must avoid dumping too large a quantity of food to avoid any risk of fatal pollution (rising nitrate levels). All food must disappear quickly.

Food plants

Being omnivorous, it is also just as possible and even advisable to provide shrimp with foods of plant origin. Although they will certainly already find happiness in a well-planted tank, by attacking moss and algae in particular, we can give them different types of plants present in our kitchens: vegetables such as zucchini, carrot (rich in beta-carotene, which strengthens colors), cucumber, spinach (rich in calcium), broccoli, salad. It is best to blanch the vegetables in boiling water for a few minutes to make them more tender.

We can also offer them pieces of fresh fruit (banana, strawberry, apple, etc.) or different leaves from the garden (nettles, dandelions, etc. also blanched), ensuring that they are not polluted by avoiding collect them near roads or agricultural fields.

As you will have understood, the possibilities are great.
However, always find out about the possible toxicity of a new food before introducing it into the aquarium.

Biofilm

The biofilm is a mixture of microorganisms composed of bacteria, protozoa, microalgae and fungi, maintained within a viscous layer forming naturally on different surfaces of the aquarium: walls, roots, stones, substrate, etc. It represents the basic natural food source for shrimps and especially juveniles.

Its development is directly dependent on the quality of the cycling and the balance of the tank (enough nutrients and good filtration/oxygenation of the water promote the development of bacteria).

If you notice the presence of biofilm in your tank, do not vacuum it up while cleaning your aquarium. You will deprive your shrimp of an interesting nutritional contribution! However, if they seem to be disinterested in it, you can of course remove it.

Not to be confused with the mycodermic film (or veil), which looks like a light white veil or an oily stain on the surface of the aquarium water, harmless to shrimp but often unsightly.

▲ Example of a root covered in a cottony white jelly: the biofilm

Care and maintenance

Maintain the aquarium

Bimonthly or even monthly maintenance will be more than sufficient to keep an aquarium containing only shrimp clean and healthy. In fact, shrimp are far from being very polluting and even already contribute to the maintenance of the tank by themselves. This will only go through a few tasks that we will describe in this part.

Controls

Controls are very important. They will consist of checking the correct temperature and the correct value of the water parameters (notably nitrates). They must be carried out regularly (once a day for temperature and at least once a month for nitrates) and during any notable change in shrimp behavior (decrease in activity, absence of reproduction, loss of appetite, attempt jumps outside the tank, etc.) The rest of the checks (once a week) will consist of inspecting the general good condition of the tank: operation of the technical equipment (pump, lighting, heating if present, etc.), the good plant growth, the absence of rot and overly invasive algae and finally the cleanliness of the water (it must be clear without any particular odor).

Cleaning

To clean any item (decorations, windows, equipment, etc.) do not use any household products. If possible, use aquarium water as the only cleaner or, failing that, tap water.

The windows

The windows can become covered with algae and various deposits. To remove them, you can use a household sponge (intended only for aquarist use), cotton wool (perlon), a cleaning magnet or a scraper intended for. It is not recommended to use white vinegar to clean any traces of limescale left by the water level. If you do this, make sure the vinegar does not leak into the aquarium and wipe with a clean cloth after the procedure.

Filtration

The filter media must never be rinsed with tap water. Chlorine would kill all the vital bacteria they contain.

Cleaning the filter media must be done at the same time as one of the water changes (see below). So, with the old water removed from the aquarium, you can rinse the filter media without any risk. It is not necessary for the masses to be as good as new when reinserted into the filter, just make sure that the bulk of the waste is removed. You can then place the filter back in the aquarium and throw away the dirty water (you can also use it to water your plants which will appreciate this quality natural fertilizer!)

Water changes

Water changes of approximately 15% every 2 weeks should be carried out, regardless of the level of apparent dirt. The latter allow the evacuation of any nitrogenous waste (especially nitrates) and preserve the balance of the aquarium.

Before any water change, you will need to ensure that you have water that has stood long enough to no longer contain chlorine (if you use piped water). If you have technical flooring, you will need to use reverse osmosis water.

Using a small siphon will allow you to suck up water and waste at the bottom of the aquarium at the same time, without disturbing your animals.

Place the end of the siphon containing the bell in the aquarium and the other end in a bucket or can. Start siphoning by pressing the bulb integrated into the siphon, then cover the entire floor by moving the bell.

▲ Technique of cleaning the floor with the bell of a siphon

Water level adjustment
In an uncovered heated aquarium, it is normal to have more or less pronounced evaporation of the aquarium water. To compensate for this loss of pure water, it is essential to top up with very soft water so as not to increase the concentration of mineral salts in the tank. For this you can use reverse osmosis water or bottled mineral water such as Mont Roucous for small volumes.

Care and maintenance

Prevention

Shrimp, like all invertebrates, are very sensitive to certain products that are extremely toxic to them. This is why before any new element is introduced into the tank, it must be ensured that it is non-dangerous.

They are particularly vulnerable to chemical products: household products obviously, but also fertilizers, pesticides, fumes and vapors from cosmetic products and in general any product likely to contain heavy metals such as copper or lead. They are also, as we have already seen, very sensitive to water pollution, particularly nitrates.

Good gestures

For any element recovered from nature and integrated into the bin, it will be necessary to ensure that the place of origin is healthy, free of any pollution.

We will thus avoid areas located near agricultural fields, wastewater treatment plants and sewer discharges or near industrial sites.

For the plants introduced after the shrimp, we ensured that they did not contain any chemical fertilizers or pesticides, favoring their purchase from specialist and reliable aquarium stores. Preferably soak them for a few days in isolated water when possible, to remove all products.

Be sure to place your bin in a room where the air is healthy and not likely to contain toxic products (perfume, deodorant, cooking grease vapor, etc.)

Carry out weekly maintenance as recommended in the section - Maintaining the bin - by siphoning off the waste on the ground as closely as possible. Also, do not hesitate to remove any remaining food that may have been uneaten after a day.

Other species

If the Neocaridina Davidi species is by far one of the best known, most popular and most suitable shrimp for beginners, it is not the only one in existence. There are other species and subspecies, with more or less different appearances and needs. This part aims to present these different shrimps succinctly in order to offer a global vision of freshwater shrimps today widespread in aquariums.

Some species presented here will also be perfectly suited to beginners, with relatively simple needs and quite similar to those of the Neocaridina Davidi. Other species will, on the contrary, be more complex and whose maintenance is not recommended for beginners. To make your perfect choice on the most suitable species according to your level and the conditions that you can offer to your future animals (aquarium volume, water parameter, etc.), we will present the needs of each species.

Caridina Multidentata

Caridina Mariae "Tiger"

Caridina Cantonensis "Pinto"

Atyopsis moluccensis

Caridina Serrata

Other species

Caridinas

Caridinas are the "richest" freshwater aquarium shrimp family in terms of subspecies. There are several dozen different ones, some of which are very simple to maintain (like the famous Caridina Multidentata shrimp, also called Amano shrimp after the famous Japanese aquascaper Takashi Amano who popularized it).

Caridinas for beginners

Among the Caridinas subspecies most accessible to beginners we find:

Caridina mariae :

"Tiger"
"Super Tiger"

Caridina Multidentata
Caridina cf. babaulti
Caridina cf breviata
Caridina cf. Simoni
Caridina sp. "Racoon Tiger"
Atyopsis moluccensis

These species support a wide range of water parameters and can grow in an aquarium with **neutral soil.**

Caridinas for confirmed

Among the most difficult Caridina subspecies to maintain and therefore not recommended for beginners:

Caridina mariae :

"Tiger orange eyes"
"Black Tiger"
"Red Tiger"

Caridina cf. Cantonensis :

"Crystal red" and "super Crystal red"
"Crystal black" and "super Crystal black"
"Taiwan bee"...
"Snow golden", "Snow white", ...

Caridina cf. serrata
Paracaridina sp

These species need precise water parameters, achievable only with the use of **aqua soil** and **osmosis water.**

Required water parameters :

pH : 5.5 to 7.5

KH: 0 to 3 (Essential, otherwise it will be impossible to molt)

GH : 2 to 6°

Caridina Multidentata

The Caridina Multidentata shrimp (also called Amano or Japonica shrimp) must have its specific part, as its historical popularity is great (even if today more and more exceeded by the Neocaridina davidi) and its needs are not always well known. aquarists, beginners or even experienced.

Size

Firstly, and unlike the Neocaridinas, the Amano shrimp is not a dwarf shrimp. As an adult, it measures between 4 and 5cm in length on average, thus requiring for their well-being a tank of at least 60 liters of volume. We then forget about their maintenance in nanoaquariums. And we are talking about maintenance and not breeding, because their second major distinction is that they cannot reproduce in fresh water.

Reproduction

If reproduction strictly speaking takes place in fresh water (mating, incubation and hatching) the larvae hatching from the eggs need to stay in brackish water (slightly salty water) just after birth to reach the juvenile stage. Once this development has passed, they must then return to fresh water.

In captivity, this process is complex to carry out both in terms of the timing of the passage of larvae from fresh water to brackish water and vice versa, as well as to obtain the appropriate water parameters (difficult salt dosage). So much so that most Amano shrimp sold commercially are mainly taken from the wild.

Behavior

Just like the Neocaridina, the Amano shrimp is gregarious. It is imperative to keep it in groups of at least 5/6 individuals and not alone or in pairs as is commonly seen. Another point of difference this time, the Amano shrimp has a tougher and less fearful character than its cousin Neocaridina. It has happened many times that she has been surprised to attack fish, especially those with sails. Hence the need to provide a tank large enough to ensure living space for everyone and peaceful cohabitation.

Other species

Synthesis

Below you will find a summary table bringing together all freshwater aquarium species and all the important and relevant information allowing their maintenance in an aquarium. It is also good to remember that mixing species/subspecies within the same tank should be avoided as much as possible in order to avoid any risk of hybridization.

Species	Origin	Water parameters			Temperature		Need		
		Ph	KH	GH	Repro	Maintenance	Volume	Sol	Repro
Neocaridina Davidi	China - Taiwan - Vietnam	6 - 8	3 - 8	5 - 15	17 - 22 °C	23 - 24 °C	25 litres	Neutral	In fresh water
Caridina Maria	China	6 - 7.5	3 - 6	3 - 12	15 - 22 °C	23 - 25 °C	25 litres	Neutral	In fresh water
Caridina multidentata	Japan Taiwan	6.5 - 7.5	2 - 8	5 - 15	18 - 22 °C	23 - 25 °C	60 litres	Neutral / Aquasoil	In fresh and brackish water
Caridina babaulti	India	6.5 - 7.5	4 - 8	8 - 15	22 - 27 °C	28 - 30 °C	25 litres	Neutral	In fresh water
Caridina breviata	South China	6 - 7.5	4 - 8	2 - 8	20 - 24 °C	25 - 26 °C	25 litres	Neutral	In fresh water
Caridina Simoni	Sri Lanka	6.5 - 7.5	2 - 8	4 - 15	18 - 24 °C	25 - 26 °C	25 litres	Neutral	In fresh water
Caridina sp. "Racoon"	Vietnam	6.5 - 7.5	2 - 4	2 - 8	20 - 24 °C	25 - 28 °C	25 litres	Neutral / Aquasoil	In fresh water
Atyopsis moluccensis	Sri Lanka to the Philippines	6.8 - 7.5	4 - 8	6 - 15	22 - 25 °C	26 - 28 °C	100 litres	Neutral	In fresh and brackish water
Caridina Maria	China	5.5 - 7.5	0 - 3	2 - 6	15 - 22 °C	23 - 25 °C	25 litres	Aquasoil	In fresh water
Caridina Cantonensis	China	6 - 7	0 - 3	2 - 6	15 - 22 °C	23 - 25 °C	25 litres	Aquasoil	In fresh water
Caridina serrata	China	6 - 7.5	0 - 3	2 - 8	18 - 23 °C	24 - 29 °C	25 litres	Aquasoil	In fresh water
Paracaridina sp.	Vietnam	6 - 7.5	0 - 3	2 - 6	17 - 22 °C	23 - 24 °C	25 litres	Aquasoil	In fresh water

The information provided in the table above represents only a preamble. They aim to help you determine which species is likely to best match your aquarium and its characteristics. In-depth and additional research will be necessary before any acquisition.

The species in green are the relatively simple species to maintain and reproduce.
The species in red are the more complicated species, not recommended if you are a beginner. In addition to the water parameters given in the table, it will be necessary to control the general conductivity of the water which must be kept relatively low (~50 µS/cm).

You now have all the information to get started in shrimp farming. We wish you a lot of fun and many pleasant hours contemplating your new aquarium and its occupant.

And if this guide has helped you, do not hesitate to let us know by leaving an opinion on the comment space accessible below.

Also discover our other works, dedicated to the world of aquariums :

See you soon.

PSSSSST !

If you have no experience of aquarium keeping and are about to embark on this wonderful world with the acquisition of aquarium shrimps, we've thought of you to make your first steps easier !

On the following pages, you'll find maintenance sheets for you to complete for the next 24 weeks. They will guide you through the maintenance tasks to be carried out, and help you keep track of the calendar. This way, you'll know exactly when and which tasks to carry out to keep your shrimp's aquarium as healthy and beautiful as your pet !

Care and maintenance

Follow-up sheet 📋

Date : ....

Water checking 💧

Temperature : .... °K   **Nitrites (NO2) :** .... mg/l

PH : ....   **Nitrates (NO3) :** .... mg/l

GH : ....   **Phosphate (PO4) :** .... mg/l

KH : ....   **CO2 / FER :** .... / .... mg/l

Water change

% of water changed : ....%   **in gallon :** .... g

Tap water : .... g   **Osmosis water :** .... g

Filtration ♻️

Cleaning :   Rinsing filter materials ☐

Replacement of filter materials ☐

MY MAINTENANCE SHEET TO CUT OUT AND STICK ON THE TANK GLASS SO YOU DON'T FORGET ANYTHING !

Last maintenance : ....

Next maintenance for : ....

To do :   Filtration ☐   Water change ☐

Glass ☐   Plants ☐

Care and maintenance

Date : ....

Water checking 💧

Temperature : .... °K   **Nitrites (NO2) :** .... mg/l

PH : ....   **Nitrates (NO3) :** .... mg/l

GH : ....   **Phosphate (PO4) :** .... mg/l

KH : ....   **CO2 / FER :** .... / .... mg/l

Water change

% of water changed : ....%   **in gallon** : .... g

Tap water : .... g   **Osmosis water :** .... g

Filtration ♻

Cleaning :   Rinsing filter materials ☐

Replacement of filter materials ☐

MY MAINTENANCE SHEET TO
CUT OUT AND STICK ON THE
TANK GLASS SO YOU DON'T
FORGET ANYTHING !

Last maintenance : ....

Next maintenance for : ....

To do :   Filtration ☐ Water change ☐

Glass ☐ Plants ☐

Care and maintenance

Date : ....

Follow-up sheet

Water checking

Temperature : .... °K   **Nitrites (NO2) :** .... mg/l

PH : ....   **Nitrates (NO3) :** .... mg/l

GH : ....   **Phosphate (PO4) :** .... mg/l

KH : ....   **CO2 / FER :** .... / .... mg/l

Water change

% of water changed : ....%   **in gallon :** .... g

Tap water : .... g   **Osmosis water :** .... g

Filtration

Cleaning :   Rinsing filter materials ☐

Replacement of filter materials ☐

MY MAINTENANCE SHEET TO CUT OUT AND STICK ON THE TANK GLASS SO YOU DON'T FORGET ANYTHING !

Last maintenance : ....

Next maintenance for : ....

To do :   Filtration ☐   Water change ☐

Glass ☐   Plants ☐

Care and maintenance

Date : ....

Follow-up sheet 📝

Water checking 💧

Temperature : .... °K	**Nitrites (NO2) :** .... mg/l
PH :	**Nitrates (NO3) :** .... mg/l
GH :	**Phosphate (PO4) :** .... mg/l
KH :	**CO2 / FER :** .... / .... mg/l

Water change

% of water changed : ....%   **in gallon**   : .... g

Tap water   : .... g   **Osmosis water :** .... g

Filtration ♻️

Cleaning :   Rinsing filter materials ☐

           Replacement of filter materials ☐

MY MAINTENANCE SHEET TO CUT OUT AND STICK ON THE TANK GLASS SO YOU DON'T FORGET ANYTHING !

Last maintenance   : ....

Next maintenance for : ....

To do :   Filtration ☐   Water change ☐
          Glass ☐   Plants ☐

Care and maintenance

Follow-up sheet

Date : ....

Water checking 💧

Temperature :	.... °K	**Nitrites (NO2) :**	.... mg/l
PH :	....	**Nitrates (NO3) :**	.... mg/l
GH :	....	**Phosphate (PO4) :**	.... mg/l
KH :	....	**CO2 / FER :**	.... / .... mg/l

Water change

% of water changed : ....%	**in gallon** : .... g
Tap water : .... g	**Osmosis water :** .... g

Filtration ♻

Cleaning :
- Rinsing filter materials ☐
- Replacement of filter materials ☐

MY MAINTENANCE SHEET TO CUT OUT AND STICK ON THE TANK GLASS SO YOU DON'T FORGET ANYTHING !

Last maintenance : ....

Next maintenance for : ....

To do : Filtration ☐ Water change ☐ Glass ☐ Plants ☐

Care and maintenance

Follow-up sheet 📋

Date : ....

Water checking 💧

Temperature : .... °K   **Nitrites (NO2) :** .... mg/l

PH : ....   **Nitrates (NO3) :** .... mg/l

GH : ....   **Phosphate (PO4) :** .... mg/l

KH : ....   **CO2 / FER :** .... / mg/l

Water change

% of water changed : ....%   **in gallon :** .... g

Tap water : .... g   **Osmosis water :** .... g

Filtration ♻

Cleaning :   Rinsing filter materials ☐

     Replacement of filter materials ☐

MY MAINTENANCE SHEET TO
CUT OUT AND STICK ON THE
TANK GLASS SO YOU DON'T
FORGET ANYTHING !

✂ - - - - - - - -

Last maintenance : ....

Next maintenance for : ....

To do :   Filtration ☐   Water change ☐

      Glass ☐   Plants ☐

Care and maintenance

Follow-up sheet

Date : ....

Water checking 💧

Temperature : .... °K   **Nitrites (NO2) :** .... mg/l

PH :   ....   **Nitrates (NO3) :** .... mg/l

GH :   ....   **Phosphate (PO4) :** .... mg/l

KH :   ....   **CO2 / FER :**   .... / .... mg/l

Water change

% of water changed : ....%   **in gallon**   : .... g

Tap water   : ....g   **Osmosis water :** .... g

Filtration ♻

Cleaning :   Rinsing filter materials   ☐

          Replacement of filter materials   ☐

MY MAINTENANCE SHEET TO
CUT OUT AND STICK ON THE
TANK GLASS SO YOU DON'T
FORGET ANYTHING !

Last maintenance   : ....

Next maintenance for : ....

To do :   Filtration ☐ Water change ☐
          Glass ☐   Plants   ☐

Care and maintenance

Date : ....

Follow-up sheet 📋

Water checking 💧

Temperature : .... °K   **Nitrites (NO2) :** .... mg/l

PH : ....   **Nitrates (NO3) :** .... mg/l

GH : ....   **Phosphate (PO4) :** .... mg/l

KH : ....   **CO2 / FER :** .... / .... mg/l

Water change

% of water changed : ....%   **in gallon :** .... g

Tap water : .... g   **Osmosis water :** .... g

Filtration ♻️

Cleaning :   Rinsing filter materials ☐

Replacement of filter materials ☐

MY MAINTENANCE SHEET TO CUT OUT AND STICK ON THE TANK GLASS SO YOU DON'T FORGET ANYTHING !

Last maintenance : ....

Next maintenance for : ....

To do :   Filtration ☐   Water change ☐

Glass ☐   Plants ☐

Care and maintenance

Date : ....

Follow-up sheet

Water checking 💧

Temperature : .... °K   **Nitrites (NO2) :** .... mg/l

PH : ....   **Nitrates (NO3) :** .... mg/l

GH : ....   **Phosphate (PO4) :** .... mg/l

KH : ....   **CO2 / FER :** ..../ .... mg/l

Water change

% of water changed : ....% **in gallon** : .... g

Tap water : .... g **Osmosis water :** .... g

Filtration ♻

Cleaning :   Rinsing filter materials   ☐

Replacement of filter materials   ☐

MY MAINTENANCE SHEET TO CUT OUT AND STICK ON THE TANK GLASS SO YOU DON'T FORGET ANYTHING !

Last maintenance : ....

Next maintenance for : ....

To do :   Filtration ☐ Water change ☐
Glass ☐ Plants ☐

Care and maintenance

Follow-up sheet

Date : ....

Water checking

Temperature : .... °K   **Nitrites (NO2) :** .... mg/l

PH : ....   **Nitrates (NO3) :** .... mg/l

GH : ....   **Phosphate (PO4) :** .... mg/l

KH : ....   **CO2 / FER :** .... / .... mg/l

Water change

% of water changed : ....%   **in gallon :** .... g

Tap water : .... g   **Osmosis water :** .... g

Filtration

Cleaning :

Rinsing filter materials ☐

Replacement of filter materials ☐

MY MAINTENANCE SHEET TO CUT OUT AND STICK ON THE TANK GLASS SO YOU DON'T FORGET ANYTHING !

Last maintenance : ....

Next maintenance for : ....

To do : Filtration ☐ Water change ☐
Glass ☐ Plants ☐

Care and maintenance

Follow-up sheet

Date : ....

Water checking

Temperature : .... °K   **Nitrites (NO2) :** .... mg/l

PH : .... **Nitrates (NO3) :** .... mg/l

GH : .... **Phosphate (PO4) :** .... mg/l

KH : .... **CO2 / FER :** .... / .... mg/l

Water change

% of water changed : ....% **in gallon** : .... g

Tap water : .... g **Osmosis water :** .... g

Filtration

Cleaning :

Rinsing filter materials ☐

Replacement of filter materials ☐

MY MAINTENANCE SHEET TO CUT OUT AND STICK ON THE TANK GLASS SO YOU DON'T FORGET ANYTHING !

Last maintenance : ....

Next maintenance for : ....

To do : Filtration ☐ Water change ☐

Glass ☐ Plants ☐

Care and maintenance

Follow-up sheet

Date : ....

Water checking 💧

Temperature : .... °K   **Nitrites (NO2) :** .... mg/l

PH : ....   **Nitrates (NO3) :** .... mg/l

GH : ....   **Phosphate (PO4) :** .... mg/l

KH : ....   **CO2 / FER :** .... / .... mg/l

Water change

% of water changed : .... %   **in gallon :** .... g

Tap water : .... g   **Osmosis water :** .... g

Filtration ♲

Cleaning :   Rinsing filter materials ☐

Replacement of filter materials ☐

MY MAINTENANCE SHEET TO CUT OUT AND STICK ON THE TANK GLASS SO YOU DON'T FORGET ANYTHING !

Last maintenance : ....

Next maintenance for : ....

To do :   Filtration ☐   Water change ☐
Glass ☐   Plants ☐

Care and maintenance

Follow-up sheet

Date : ....

Water checking 💧

Temperature : .... °K	**Nitrites (NO2) :** .... mg/l
PH :	**Nitrates (NO3) :** .... mg/l
GH :	**Phosphate (PO4) :** .... mg/l
KH :	**CO2 / FER :** .... / .... mg/l

Water change

% of water changed : ....%   **in gallon**   : .... g

Tap water   : .... g   **Osmosis water :** .... g

Filtration ♻

Cleaning :

Rinsing filter materials ☐

Replacement of filter materials ☐

MY MAINTENANCE SHEET TO CUT OUT AND STICK ON THE TANK GLASS SO YOU DON'T FORGET ANYTHING !

Last maintenance   : ....

Next maintenance for : ....

To do :   Filtration ☐   Water change ☐

       Glass ☐   Plants ☐

Care and maintenance

Follow-up sheet

Date : ....

Water checking 💧

Temperature : .... °K   **Nitrites (NO2) :** .... mg/l

PH : ....   **Nitrates (NO3) :** .... mg/l

GH : ....   **Phosphate (PO4) :** .... mg/l

KH : ....   **CO2 / FER :** .... / .... mg/l

Water change

% of water changed : .... %   **in gallon** : .... g

Tap water : .... g   **Osmosis water :** .... g

Filtration ♲

Cleaning :   Rinsing filter materials ☐

Replacement of filter materials ☐

MY MAINTENANCE SHEET TO CUT OUT AND STICK ON THE TANK GLASS SO YOU DON'T FORGET ANYTHING !

Last maintenance : ....

Next maintenance for : ....

To do :   Filtration ☐   Water change ☐

Glass ☐   Plants ☐

Care and maintenance

Follow-up sheet

Date : ....

Water checking

Temperature : .... °K	Nitrites (NO2) : .... mg/l
PH :	Nitrates (NO3) : .... mg/l
GH :	Phosphate (PO4) : .... mg/l
KH :	CO2 / FER : .... / .... mg/l

---

Water change

% of water changed : ....%   in gallon   : .... g

Tap water   : .... g   Osmosis water : .... g

---

Filtration

Cleaning :

Rinsing filter materials ☐

Replacement of filter materials ☐

MY MAINTENANCE SHEET TO CUT OUT AND STICK ON THE TANK GLASS SO YOU DON'T FORGET ANYTHING !

Last maintenance : ....

Next maintenance for : ....

To do :
Filtration ☐   Water change ☐
Glass ☐   Plants ☐

Care and maintenance

Follow-up sheet

Date : ....

Water checking

Temperature : .... °K   **Nitrites (NO2) :** .... mg/l

PH : ....   **Nitrates (NO3) :** .... mg/l

GH : ....   **Phosphate (PO4) :** .... mg/l

KH : ....   **CO2 / FER :** .... / .... mg/l

Water change

% of water changed : .... %   **in gallon :** .... g

Tap water : .... g   **Osmosis water :** .... g

Filtration

Cleaning :

Rinsing filter materials ☐

Replacement of filter materials ☐

MY MAINTENANCE SHEET TO CUT OUT AND STICK ON THE TANK GLASS SO YOU DON'T FORGET ANYTHING !

Last maintenance : ....

Next maintenance for : ....

To do : Filtration ☐ Water change ☐

Glass ☐ Plants ☐

Care and maintenance

Follow-up sheet

Date : ....

Water checking 💧

Temperature : .... °K   **Nitrites (NO2) :** .... mg/l

PH :   ....   **Nitrates (NO3) :** .... mg/l

GH :   ....   **Phosphate (PO4) :** .... mg/l

KH :   ....   **CO2 / FER :** .... / .... mg/l

Water change

% of water changed : ....%   in gallon   : .... g

Tap water   : .... g   Osmosis water : .... g

Filtration ♻

Cleaning :   Rinsing filter materials   ☐

           Replacement of filter materials   ☐

MY MAINTENANCE SHEET TO
CUT OUT AND STICK ON THE
TANK GLASS SO YOU DON'T
FORGET ANYTHING !

Last maintenance   : ....

Next maintenance for : ....

To do :   Filtration ☐   Water change ☐

         Glass ☐   Plants ☐

Care and maintenance

Follow-up sheet

Date : ....

Water checking 💧

Temperature : .... °K   **Nitrites (NO2) :** .... mg/l

PH : ....   **Nitrates (NO3) :** .... mg/l

GH : ....   **Phosphate (PO4) :** .... mg/l

KH : ....   **CO2 / FER :** .... / .... mg/l

Water change

% of water changed : .... %   **in gallon :** .... g

Tap water : .... g   **Osmosis water :** .... g

Filtration ♺

Cleaning :   Rinsing filter materials ☐

   Replacement of filter materials ☐

MY MAINTENANCE SHEET TO CUT OUT AND STICK ON THE TANK GLASS SO YOU DON'T FORGET ANYTHING !

Last maintenance : ....

Next maintenance for : ....

To do :   Filtration ☐   Water change ☐

   Glass ☐   Plants ☐

Care and maintenance

Follow-up sheet

Date : ....

Water checking 💧

Temperature : .... °K	**Nitrites (NO2) :** .... mg/l
PH :	**Nitrates (NO3) :** .... mg/l
GH :	**Phosphate (PO4) :** .... mg/l
KH :	**CO2 / FER :** .... / mg/l

Water change

% of water changed : ....%   **in gallon**   **:** .... g

Tap water   **:** .... g   **Osmosis water :** .... g

Filtration ♻

Cleaning :

Rinsing filter materials ☐

Replacement of filter materials ☐

MY MAINTENANCE SHEET TO CUT OUT AND STICK ON THE TANK GLASS SO YOU DON'T FORGET ANYTHING !

Last maintenance   : ....

Next maintenance for : ....

To do :   Filtration ☐ Water change ☐

   Glass ☐ Plants ☐

Care and maintenance

Follow-up sheet

Date : ....

Water checking

Temperature : .... °K   **Nitrites (NO2) :** .... mg/l

PH : ....   **Nitrates (NO3) :** .... mg/l

GH : ....   **Phosphate (PO4) :** .... mg/l

KH : ....   **CO2 / FER :** .... / .... mg/l

Water change

% of water changed : ....%   **in gallon** : .... g

Tap water : .... g   **Osmosis water :** .... g

Filtration

Cleaning :   Rinsing filter materials   ☐

Replacement of filter materials   ☐

MY MAINTENANCE SHEET TO CUT OUT AND STICK ON THE TANK GLASS SO YOU DON'T FORGET ANYTHING !

Last maintenance   : ....

Next maintenance for : ....

To do :   Filtration ☐ Water change ☐

Glass ☐ Plants ☐

Care and maintenance

Date : ....

Follow-up sheet 📋

Water checking 💧

Temperature :	.... °K	**Nitrites (NO2) :**	.... mg/l
PH :	....	**Nitrates (NO3) :**	.... mg/l
GH :	....	**Phosphate (PO4) :**	.... mg/l
KH :	....	**CO2 / FER :**	.... / .... mg/l

Water change

% of water changed : ....% **in gallon** : .... g

Tap water : .... g **Osmosis water :** .... g

Filtration ♻

Cleaning : Rinsing filter materials ☐

Replacement of filter materials ☐

MY MAINTENANCE SHEET TO CUT OUT AND STICK ON THE TANK GLASS SO YOU DON'T FORGET ANYTHING !

✂

Last maintenance : ....

Next maintenance for : ....

To do : Filtration ☐ Water change ☐

Glass ☐ Plants ☐

Care and maintenance

Follow-up sheet

Date : ....

Water checking

Temperature : .... °K   **Nitrites (NO2) :** .... mg/l

PH : ....   **Nitrates (NO3) :** .... mg/l

GH : ....   **Phosphate (PO4) :** .... mg/l

KH : ....   **CO2 / FER :** .... / .... mg/l

Water change

% of water changed : ....%   **in gallon :** .... g

Tap water : .... g   **Osmosis water :** .... g

Filtration

Cleaning :   Rinsing filter materials ☐

Replacement of filter materials ☐

MY MAINTENANCE SHEET TO CUT OUT AND STICK ON THE TANK GLASS SO YOU DON'T FORGET ANYTHING !

Last maintenance : ....

Next maintenance for : ....

To do :   Filtration ☐   Water change ☐

Glass ☐   Plants ☐

Care and maintenance

Date : ....

Follow-up sheet 📋

Water checking 💧

Temperature : .... °K   Nitrites (NO2) : .... mg/l

PH : ....   Nitrates (NO3) : .... mg/l

GH : ....   Phosphate (PO4) : .... mg/l

KH : ....   CO2 / FER : .... / .... mg/l

Water change

% of water changed : ....%   in gallon : .... g

Tap water : .... g   Osmosis water : .... g

Filtration ♻️

Cleaning :   Rinsing filter materials ☐

Replacement of filter materials ☐

MY MAINTENANCE SHEET TO CUT OUT AND STICK ON THE TANK GLASS SO YOU DON'T FORGET ANYTHING !

Last maintenance : ....

Next maintenance for : ....

To do : Filtration ☐ Water change ☐

Glass ☐ Plants ☐

Printed in Great Britain
by Amazon

62454653R00047